FOUNDATION
MAGIC

A Rug Hooker's Guide to Preparing Patterns

BY VICTORIA L. RUDOLPH

Presented by

R·U·G
HOOKING

Ampry Publishing, Northbrook, Illinois

Printed in the United States of America
10 9 8 7 6 5 4 3 2 1

Rug photography by the author unless otherwise noted
Cataloging-in-Publication Data
Library of Congress Control Number: 2021935509

ISBN 978-1-945550-52-2

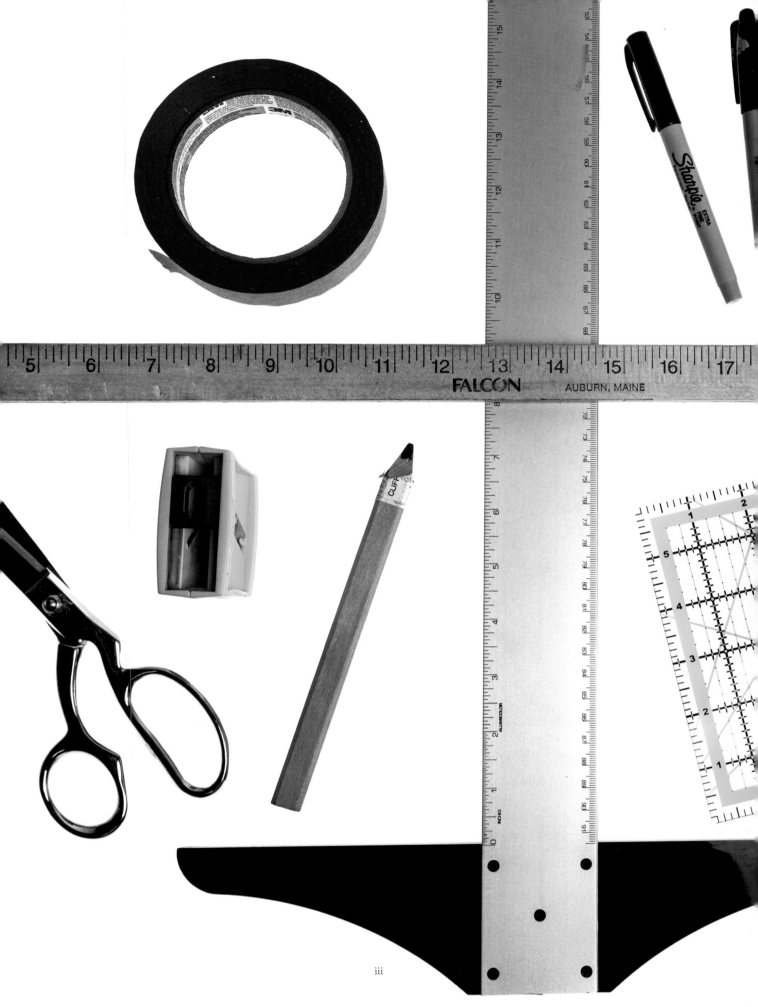

CONTENTS

Part III - Projects 34

INTRODUCTION

Rug hooking is a versatile artisan craft. These days we see a resurgence in rug making, with not only traditional methods but newer, more contemporary styles and expression. Rug hooking is becoming accepted as fine art, including hooked sculpture. We can often find finished pieces in craft and art museums around the country.

There are many types of beautiful patterns to purchase from a myriad of sources and I enjoy working on these. As an artist, however, I also like to create my own designs.

Why MAGIC? When I first started writing this book, I had no idea what to call it. Like everyone else, we were in lock down during the pandemic and I decided to use this time to write; I also decided that to energize long days of sitting at a computer and to reward myself for hard work on this book I would take long hikes along the coastal trail at the end of the day. Not only did engaging with nature help relieve the stress of the pandemic, it also helped me clear my mind and allowed me to think about this book and my rug designs. Each day I was inspired by what I saw in nature.

Like everyone else, I could not control what was going on in the world, but I could use that time to be clear my mind. The more I walked along the coast and along the wooded paths, the easier it was to relax. I discovered I was filled with creative ideas. I was able to use this time to embrace myself in creative space.

Designing and laying out rug-hooking patterns is not magic. It is an easy process which takes less time than saying ABRACADABRA. You don't have to be a magician to create a magically beautiful rug—all you need is the proper tools, a little knowledge, and creativity.

Designing a rug may seem to be intimidating, something you are reluctant to jump into. But you don't need to be an artist to create your own designs or to lay out the patterns on foundation cloth. I enjoy the process of laying out my designs on foundation cloth to prepare for rug hooking. It is exciting to see a finished piece and know you own it—start to finish.

Unless you have taken a workshop in designing your own patterns, you may not know much about the very first steps of preparing a pattern. You will find that little is written on the subject of preparing foundation. This book describes the fundamental process, methods, and equipment necessary to lay out your design to prepare it for rug hooking.

Designing your own rug pattern is fulfilling and rewarding. However, it is important to do it properly. You will be spending many hours, and possibly many dollars, to create this rug, so you must have a solid beginning with a design on backing to get you off on a good start. A well-planned design properly transferred onto the backing is critical.

This process is equally as important as picking the wools and fibers you want to use in your hooked project. It starts with knowing how to use the tools available. I learned the hard way—which is why I want to show you how to do it properly. The little bit of extra time you invest in this step will save you time, money, and frustration. Knowing what tools to use to facilitate this and the steps in laying out your pattern will prepare the rug for hooking. The rest is up to you.

There are several special terms in this book that are intended to help you navigate this process more smoothly.

This book will demonstrate how to prepare your foundation cloth for several different projects. These include tile-inspired rugs, student kits, a coat of arms, a tree skirt, clothing, sculpture, and landscapes.

Alan's Mountain Rug, *36" x 24", wool on linen. Designed and hooked by Victoria L. Rudolph, 2005. This was my very first rug and my own design, created for my husband's office. Dixie Coyle, my first rug-hooking teacher, showed me how to lay this design out on the foundation cloth and guided me with the color planning. My bright color palette preference has not changed in 16 years of rug hooking.*

I have been an artist all my life, but it wasn't until I was introduced to the art of rug hooking that I finally found "my thang." As a child, I was encouraged to use my imagination. If I wasn't drawing, I was trying to make something with fiber and textiles. I was taught to sew by hand at an early age. Growing up in New York City, I was exposed to many different forms of art with trips to the museums, street art shows, and art classes.

I was also inspired by my mother, who would sew costumes for school plays and Halloween. She ran our school's holiday fair for many years, and she would sit and make doll beds out of donated cigar boxes, textiles, and clothespins. The beds were first painted, and then filled with a handmade mattress, duvet cover, and pillows. Sometime she would knit or crochet a little blanket and she would often make matching canopies. When I look back on those days, I wish we had known about rug hooking because I bet my mother would have made some beautiful rugs!

When I started rug hooking in 2005, my husband surprised me at the holidays with a Townsend wool cutter. I also surprised him with my very first designed

rug, which is still in use today. Dixie Coyle, my dear friend and rug hooking teacher in Steamboat Springs, Colorado, taught me how to prepare the linen and draw my design.

Later in graduate school, when I had to choose a thesis for my MFA, I proposed combining two mediums, painting and rug hooking, to demonstrate how one could transfer nicely to another. Each followed a similar process and, in my mind, they were a natural pairing.

I spent the last 18 months of school planning and painting 12 pieces, each with its matching hooked rug

counterpart. It was quite an undertaking but worth every minute. No one had ever asked to do their thesis in rug hooking. The school wanted one of my pieces for their collection; it was hanging on the department walls until the COVID-19 pandemic, when everything was shut down. My piece is now hanging in the Administrator's home office; she occasionally sends me photos to remind me it is safe. It is things like this small act of kindness on her part that makes me so proud of this medium.

PART I
TOOLS & METHODS

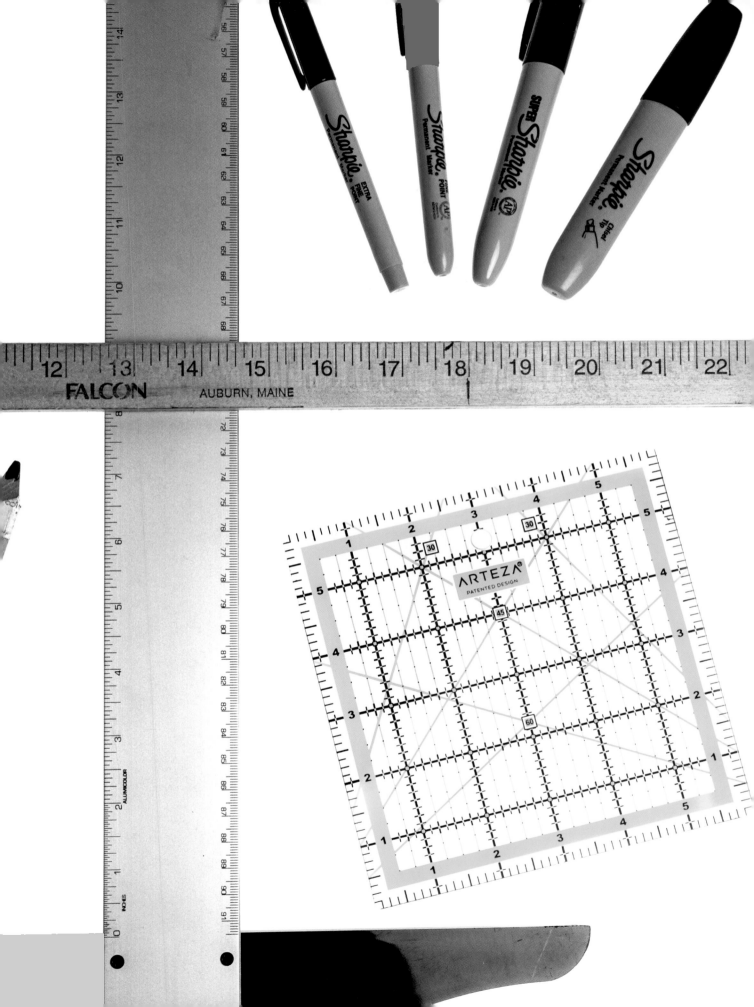

Not everyone has access to a wonderful teacher like Dixie to show them how to lay out a rug, which is why, after creating many of my own patterns, I decided to write a book about this fundamental process. This process is equally as important as picking the wools and fibers you want to use in your hooked project. It starts with knowing how to use the tools available. The little bit of extra effort you invest in this step will save you time, money, and frustration. Knowing which tools to use and the steps to follow in laying out your pattern will prepare the rug for hooking. The rest is up to you.

Foundation Cloth

In order to lay out your pattern, you must first understand which items are needed. Here is the first question: What type of foundation cloth are you planning to use? There are several types available and each one is different.

Foundation cloth is the substrate on which you will draw the design and hook the rug. It is available in bleached primitive linen, unbleached primitive linen, mixed primitive linen, and traditional linen. There is also monk's cloth and rug warp. You can order these online through several rug hooking suppliers. Let's look at each of these types of foundation and the pros and cons of each.

Monk's cloth is a 100% cotton cloth. It is softer and more loosely woven (24 or 26 threads per inch) than other types of foundation cloth. It is usually a whitish color with a white woven line through it. The nice feature of this foundation cloth is that this white line makes it easy to lay out a pattern squarely.

Rug warp or warp cloth is made from a heavier 100% cotton with a stiffer weave, 11 threads x 13 threads per inch. Because it is stiffer, you need to make sure that you draw your lines evenly. The advantage is that it is made for the floor and won't "wrinkle." Also this style foundation cloth is made for smaller #3 and #4 cut strips. It is great for more detailed rugs, but more and more primitive hookers are experimenting with it and are coming to prefer the tight weave for their projects.

Many rug hookers use linen. Linen is made from the flax plant, and most linen is very flexible. There are several types available today, and your choice really depends on personal preference. Rug hooking linen is woven with 12 x 12 threads per inch and is made from 2-ply linen yarn.

Primitive natural linen is made primarily for larger cuts. Bleached primitive linen is a white linen. All hook the same. Some rug hookers prefer the bleached because they want to see their pattern on a lighter background. The regular non-bleached linen is darker and some people prefer this. Mixed linen was actually a manufacturing mistake but has turned out to be a popular middle-toned linen for those who prefer their linen to be neither too light nor too dark.

Traditional linen is also made from 2-ply threads but it is a tighter weave (13 x 13 threads per inch) and is popular for smaller #3, 4, and 5 cuts. It is the color of natural linen.

I have tried them all the different foundation fabrics and my personal preference is unbleached primitive linen or monk's cloth. The only way to decide is try them all.

Linen

Monk's cloth

Rug warp

Some people even use burlap or hessian fabric as a foundation cloth. Burlap is made from the skin of the jute plant or fibers of sisal, which is really an agave plant. I personally don't enjoy working with burlap or sisal because they are rough and scratchy, but some people prefer this style foundation cloth.

Burlap

The nice thing about all these fibers is that they are made from natural materials and work well with wool to create sturdy rugs you can throw on the floor. A well-made rug on a sturdy foundation will last for years. Linen tends to last longer than burlap.

One of the first decisions you will have when you want to lay out your pattern is to determine what size you want it to be. Some foundation cloths are wider than others, and it is critical to make sure you are getting the correct width or length for your project. The companies that sell these products will post the sizes on their websites and will often have someone who can help you determine what size you need.

If you are designing patterns for sale, you will probably want to purchase a bolt of foundation cloth from the vendor rather than ordering separate sizes. This will help keep your costs down, especially if you are planning on creating multiples of one design or if you intend to sell these patterns to the public.

Tools

You will need a yardstick or T-square, a dry flat surface or sturdy wide table, and a light table, lightbox, or the window. For marking, you will need a construction pencil and construction pencil sharpener, scissors, black permanent markers, drywall mesh fabric and/or transfer cloth like red-dot fabric. To finish the edges, a serger is handy though not necessary.

Light Pads, Lightboxes, Light Tables, Windows

As a young artist I was taught how to use a light box. I started my art career as a trained calligrapher and I needed the light box to see line guides for my work. Over the years I have owned several different sizes.

A plexiglass sheet is an excellent cover for a lightbox. It allows the perfect amount of light to come through the layers of the pattern, the foundation cloth, and the transfer material.

Manufactured light pads come in a variety of smaller sizes.
They are easy to locate in art and craft stores or on the internet at affordable prices.

A lightbox is an extremely useful tool. They are relatively inexpensive and, with advanced technology, they are now made flat.

This allows for easy storage and it is easier on your arms. My old one is simply a metal box with a metal arm, and it can be uncomfortable to use for any length of time.

Today I have a light table made especially for me, relatively inexpensively, by a handyman. I told him the size I wanted, and he constructed it with raw wood from the lumberyard. He also drilled a hole into the side for an outlet cord and added a lip around the inside of the top to hold a piece of plexiglass for the cover. I chose a mildly cloudy white plexiglass meant for a lighting system.

The entire project cost me less than $300 (the same price as a nice pattern kit with wool). I painted it with a glossy white paint. Then I purchased LED tube lighting on the internet; it came with extension connecting cords and braces. I screwed the braces into the bottom of the table and connected several of the tubes together so I could have equally and evenly distributed light throughout the box. These added tweaks allow me to draw out larger patterns with ease.

If you don't have a light pad, lightbox, or light table or if you don't own a clear glass table, don't fret. There is a simple, no-cost solution: You can hang your foundation cloth on a window with masking or painter's tape and then trace your pattern using the light coming in through the window.

Except for the foundation fabric and the plastic acrylic cover sheet, all these items are available at your local hardware store. The plastic supply store cut the plexiglass to size to fit perfectly in the top of my lightbox.

Lightbox in the corner

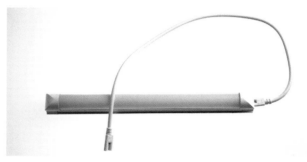
Lighting element for light box

Lightbox interior with lights connected and illuminated

Lightbox corner with corner lip exposed

Lightbox plexiglass

Tracing elephant on window pane

Rulers, T-squares, Templates

If you are cutting linen and drawing out your own pattern, it is important to have good-quality rulers that can fit the length or width of your foundation cloth. You can purchase yardsticks at most stores that sell fabric. Use these to count off yards as you measure out cloth. Yardsticks are good for making straight edges as you draw lines on your foundation cloth.

In art school before computers were widely used, we were required to use a T-square ruler to make sure we were drawing straight lines. This is especially helpful when adding a border or lettering. These tools help transfer your pattern properly. Clear quilting grid rulers are also nice because you can see what you are doing through the rulers. This is especially helpful as you line up corners. They are convenient to use and come in many sizes.

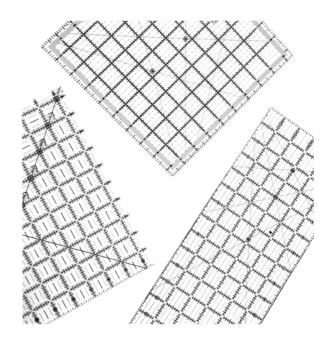

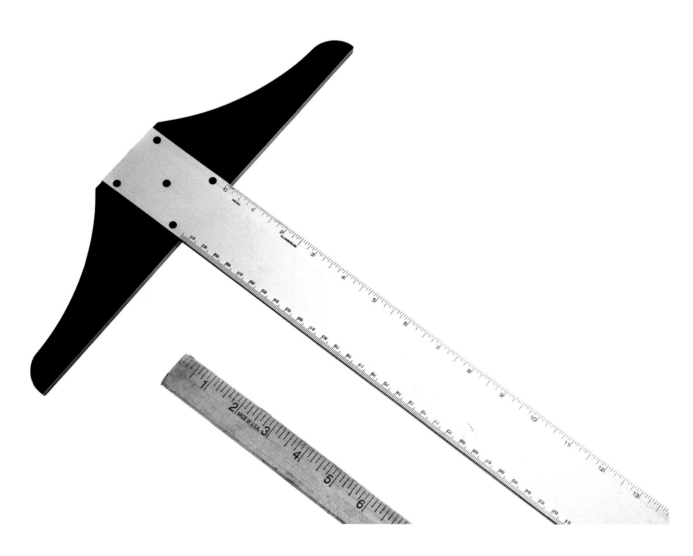

What about circles? Even as an artist I find drawing the perfect circle challenging. I will often use circle templates to help me navigate this process.

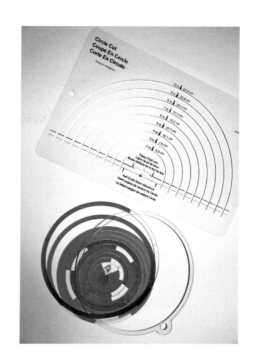

Construction Pencil

You've seen them. A construction pencil is a rectangular flat pencil that needs its own sharpener. To use the sharpener, insert the pencil sideways, which is the only way it will fit, and slide the pencil back and forth until you get the desired pencil tip. This is not like a regular pencil sharpener, so you might not get the same sharp tip as you would on a regular #2 pencil.

If you don't have a sharpener for construction pencils, you can use an artist's knife or small, sharp knife to carve the wood off the sides to form a new point. I find it easier to use the sharpener.

The benefit to using this pencil is that it forces a straight line on to the linen and doesn't leave a huge mark. I use this pencil to lay out my center lines and to help me draw straight lines in the ditch of the fabric.

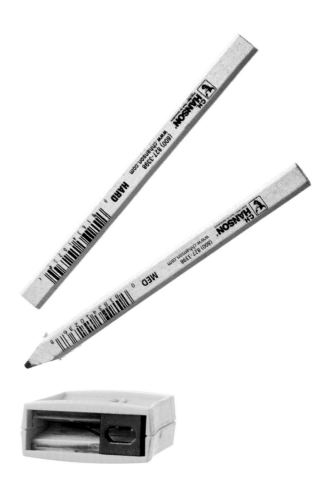

Permanent Markers

To draw your pattern, I recommend using Sharpie™ black permanent markers. These last a long time and come in a variety of widths and shapes.

Keep a supply of these markers available; it can easily happen that one runs out of ink or a tip gets ruined. Sometimes, when drawing on linen or other foundation cloth, the ink is absorbed into the fabric and the pen gets worn out quickly on the rough fibers.

I do not recommend using other colors of markers as you draw on the foundation cloth because they can bleed into your wool. Instead, use special markers designed for fabric, that are made to last and don't run. I learned this the hard way: I once color planned an entire piece with different colored permanent markers on a foundation cloth. The ink from the foundation cloth bled onto my light background wool.

Scissors

These are essential: You need a good, sharp pair of 8" fabric scissors to cut the backing cloth to the size you desire. Scissors are available almost everywhere and some stores provide sharpening services. Do not use your good fabric scissors to cut anything other than fabric. Using your good scissors on paper or another material will dull them quickly. I use a pair of 5" bent scissors to trim my wool strips. The proper technique to cut the foundation cloth will be discussed later in the book.

Transfer Tools

Tracing paper comes in a variety of brands and sizes. These papers are available at many art stores. You can also use drywall crack repair cloth or red-dot transfer fabric.

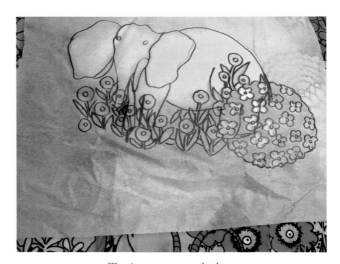

Tracing paper on elephant

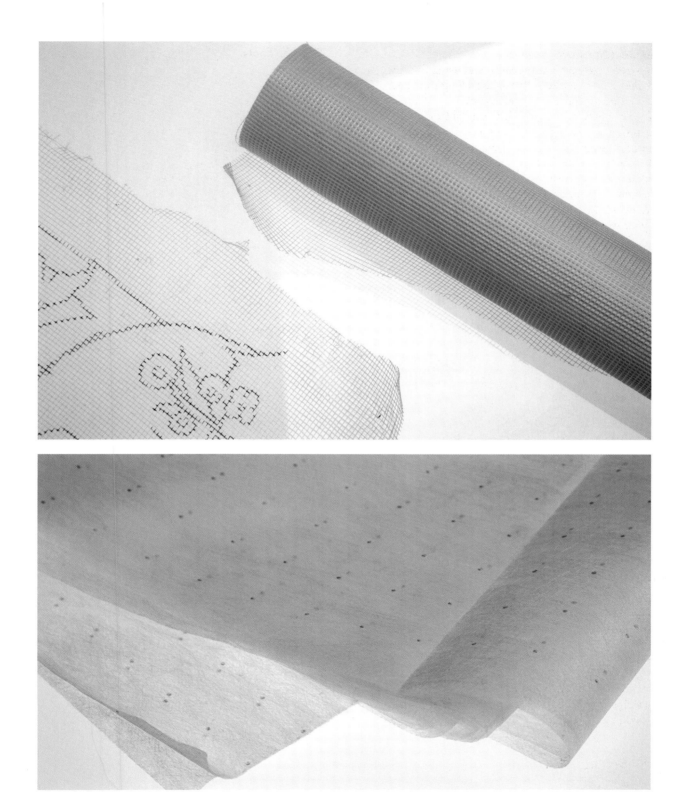

Top: Drywall crack repair material, laid over elephant design
Bottom: Red-dot transfer fabric

I love the drywall crack repair material because it is a gridded mesh that sticks to the foundation cloth and doesn't slip. It also is thick enough so that the pen doesn't run through the foundation cloth to the table beneath it. And the thickness and durability allows me to use it several times without wearing out the pen. It is woven but has larger squares than the foundation cloth, so you can line it up with the holes in the foundation cloth.

Preparing the Foundation Cloth

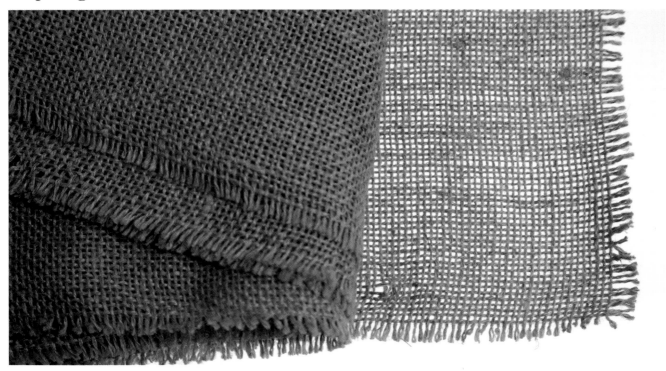

Now that you have all of your tools ready, you are ready to lay out your first pattern.

1. On a flat surface, lay out the foundation cloth.
2. Determine the size of the rug you want to hook. Start with a large piece of foundation cloth so that you have room to maneuver.
3. Add 4 to 6 inches to the dimension of each side. This will give you enough room around the design to place your piece on a hooking frame. It is difficult to hook a rug if there is not sufficient blank areas surrounding the design.
4. Mark the size of the hooked area with the permanent marker or construction pencil.

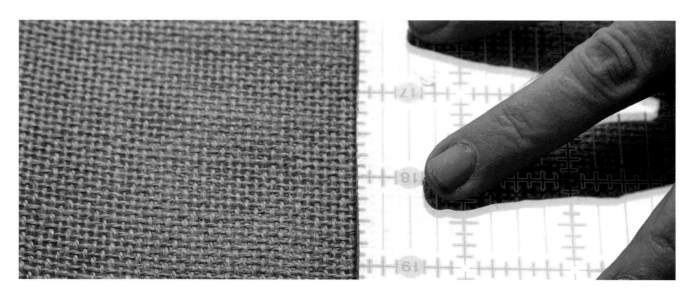

Template on foundation cloth

5. If using monk's cloth or rug warp, cut the fabric on the line you draw, making sure that it includes the extra 4" to 6" surround.

6. If using linen, very gently pull two strands of the foundation cloth along each of the drawn lines. Pull the strands out to the end so that the cloth buckles lightly.

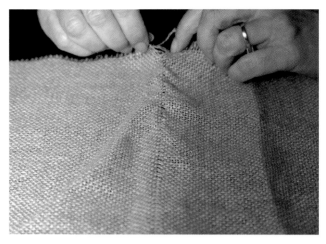

7. Then, with your scissors, cut these at the edge and gently pull the strands out. On a flat surface, lay out the foundation cloth.

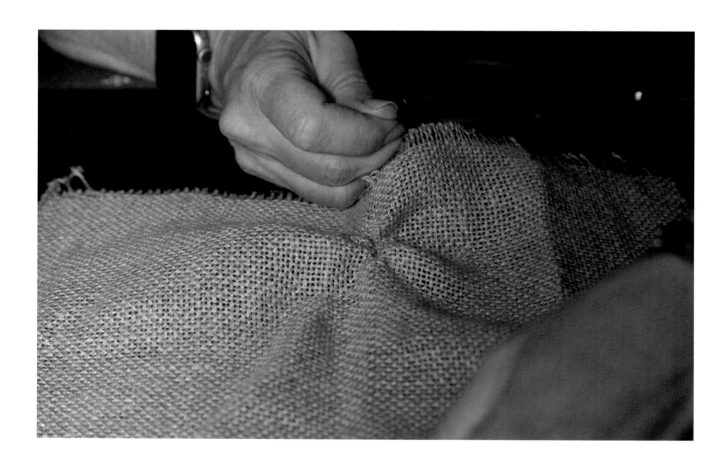

The pulled thread makes a straight line for cutting.

Carefully cutting along the pulled thread line

Transferring the Pattern

1. Mark the center: Fold the foundation cloth in half and mark the center with either a construction pencil or permanent marker.

Then fold it over again so you have a crossed line exactly in the middle. Reopen this and press down the folded edges with your hands. This will be the center of your pattern. Draw a small cross where the folded lines meet, in between 2 strands of linen (called the ditch).

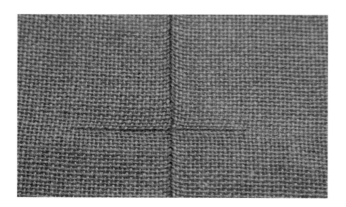

2. Using a permanent marker, draw the outline border of the rug, allowing at least 6 inches as a perimeter border. Square up the edges of the pattern to make sure it is centered and straight.

3. Place the center of your transfer pattern sheet on to the foundation cloth. Line up the center of the paper pattern with the center cross you just marked on the cloth. Then, using the permanent marker, trace along the edges of your pattern for your border line.

4. Once you are happy with how it lines up, transfer the remainder of the pattern.

Protecting the Edges

When you have completed transferring or drawing out your pattern, you need to keep the edges of the foundation cloth from fraying or unraveling. You can accomplish this in several ways.

1. Serge the edges. Using a serger, sew the edges of the foundation cloth all the way around, unless you have a selvage side.

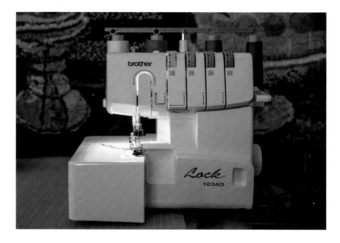

This is the method I prefer. Sergers come in several shapes and sizes and range in cost from $200 to $3,000. The one I own is easy to set up and use. I always serge the edges of the foundation cloth because the serger cuts away the loose edges, giving my foundation cloth a finished, more professional look.

2. Fold over the edges. Fold 1" of the foundation edge over on itself and sew a straight or running stitch to secure the edges. This can be done by hand or machine.

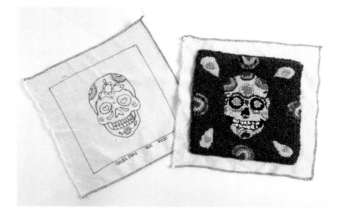

Skull pattern and hooked rug with serged line

3. Liquid sealant. Apply a sealant to all of the edges of the foundation cloth. Be sure to wait until it dries before you proceed. You may still need to sew the edges afterwards, depending on how well the sealant works.

4. Masking or painter's tape. Encase the outside edge in tape so that it does not unravel.

When I first started laying out my own patterns, I sewed my edges by hand or used masking tape. These are both acceptable methods. However, I discovered that using tape may cause a problem; it is often difficult to remove the tape without fraying the edges. This was especially challenging when I wanted to finish the edges. They never came out quite straight enough. Hand sewing the edge took me a long time and I had to allow for the edge to be rolled under when planning my finishing. Then I discovered how to use a serger. This method saved me hours of time. My serger sits out, ready to use in my studio.

There is one more step you might want consider before you start hooking your pattern. The beloved and admired Canadian rug hooker Doris Eaton has a YouTube video on how to prebind your rug with binding tape before you start the hooking. You prebind right after you transfer the pattern onto the foundation cloth. If you are going to use binding tape rather than whipstitch or use another type of finishing style, I recommend Doris Eaton's method. You might be able to still find her YouTube video. If not, the steps are simple.

Binding tape

1. In your bobbin, use a thread color that contrasts with your foundation cloth. Sew your binding tape, or the fabric that you are using as binding, "as close as you can get" to the edge border line, using right angles at the corners. Do NOT start on the corner. Start in the middle of the side of the rug border. This can be done either by machine or hand. If using a sewing machine, use your regular zipper foot. When you come to the corner turn your needle down and make a right turn. Make sure that you keep the corners turned up.

2. When you come to the end of the binding tape, turn over the edge of the end piece at an angle and sew it to the starting edge of the piece.

3. Turn over your foundation cloth and hook a line on the back side right next to the line you sewed. Now when you finish the rug it will be easy to turn over this rug binding and the corners will look neat . I have used this method many times and it has saved me hours of trouble. It also helps the rug lay flat on the floor, and the binding tape wears beautifully. Binding tape comes in many colors and can be found at most rug hooking suppliers.

TROUBLESHOOTING

What happens if you have just enough linen to hook the pattern and not enough for the overhang? It will be challenging to hook the pattern if you cannot easily put the pattern in your hooking frame. Here is one solution: sew another piece of fabric or wool around the perimeter of the foundation cloth with enough width and length to meet the 4"-6" overhang.

But the best decision? Save the too-small foundation cloth to use it for another, smaller pattern.

Piecing Foundation Cloth

Have you ever wanted to make a large rug but can't find your favorite foundation cloth in the right width? Don't worry, there is a solution. It is not difficult, but you need to know a few tricks to make it work.

Foundation cloth is limited in length and size. If you want to create a rug that is wider than 60" linen or 75" monk's cloth, you will need to sew pieces together to create the width and length you need. You must do this before you draw out your pattern. It is critical that you sew the pieces together precisely so that your hooking lines match up.

I will show you how to connect two pieces of foundation. I use the methods that I show here. You may need many pieces, depending on how large you want your rug. Invest in good brand of strong rug repair thread.

I prefer to use a heavy poly-cotton rug warp thread. You can order this online from any rug repair manufacturer, but my favorite place is HM Nabavian in New York. *(HMNabavian.com)*

If I can't get my favorite thread, I will use a heavy cotton floss thread instead.

My "go to" thread is heavy poly-cotton rug warp thread.

Two pieces of linen, overlapped and showing the line.

1. Lay out the foundation cloth on an ironing board and iron out the creases.

2. Lay the ironed pieces on a flat surface, side by side. Then take the edge of one of the pieces and place it over the edge of the other piece by about 1". If you have cloth off the bolt with selvages, use the selvage edges. This prevents the cloth from fraying.

3. Using a construction pencil, draw a straight line through each piece of foundation cloth. I usually start at the bottom. Repeat these lines on both pieces. Then pin the two pieces together, overlapping the pieces about 1" all the way up the length of the foundation cloth. *(See page 20.)*

4. Make sure your lines overlap to keep the pieces straight. If you see that the holes don't line up, that tells you that one side is incorrect and you need to remeasure and adjust.

5. Cut a length of thread that measures from your elbow to the tip of your longest finger. This will help prevent knots or tangles in your thread.

6. I use a large tapestry needle size with an eye wide enough for the repair thread and a blunt tip for comfort. The warp on linen is wide enough for this type of needle. Thread the needle and tie a knot on the end.

7. Starting at one end of the fabric, sew the pieces together in a straight line. You can either use a running basting stitch or just a running stitch, but make sure your stitches are the same length and distance so the two pieces don't bunch or snag. There are plenty of YouTube videos that provide sewing instructions and demonstrate these stitches.

8. After the two pieces are sewn together, press the seam open and flat with an iron. I will often add a liquid sealant where the edges meet to guarantee it doesn't fray.

Sewing the pieces together

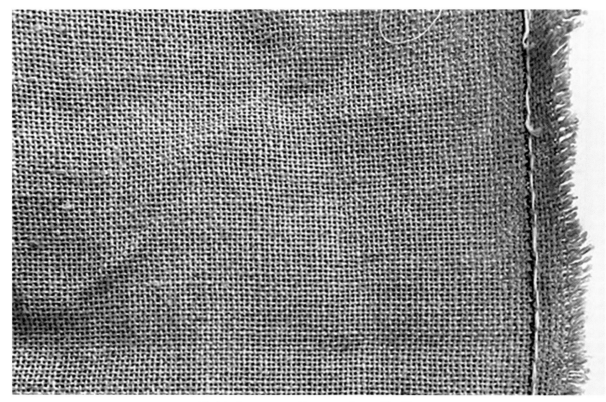

Finished seam, attaching two pieces of backing

Knotted and woven thread to secure when the piecing is completed

Pieced linen, showing the pressed seam

PART II
CREATIVITY AND YOU
DEVELOP YOUR OWN PROCESS

As a professionally-trained artist, I know how important it is to keep my creative mind active. I work at this constantly. I sketch, journal, and rug hook every day. I usually sketch 15-30 minutes a day. I carry a sketch book with me all the time, and it often includes journaled notes with dates. I also include doodling that I do while on a phone call. Sometimes those little subconscious mark-makings can turn into a wonderful motif or can lead to the creation of an entire design series.

I might add a picture I have seen in a magazine or jot down a quote or theme that intrigues me. I might write notes on a photo I have taken, and that also goes into the sketch book.

It is amazing how something I sketched or journaled in the past will inspire me for a new project or help me solve a problem I am encountering with a rug or painting. These days, if you have a tablet device, you can actually draw digitally and color plan at the same time. I use both paper journals and electronic tablets. Sometimes I just need that tactile relationship of pen to paper but I also find relaxation in using a tablet while I am in a waiting room for an appointment.

I also make a point of taking someone else's rug hooking class or art class once a month to learn something new. The only way to continue to grow as an artist is to keep learning and trying new things. During the pandemic shutdown, not only did I teach online classes, I also made time to take other artists' classes. I had time on my hands and I wanted to keep my mind flowing.

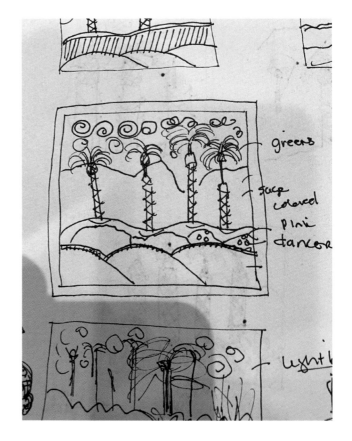

If I am not working on a specific rug, I might practice new techniques. This helps me relax and allows me to visually record my ideas. Sometimes I doodle when I am on the phone, and I often find that this subconscious mark making becomes the start of a new painting or hooked project. I keep a notebook of inspiring ideas and color combinations I may find in a printed publication. I follow other artists on Pinterest and Instagram.

Finding inspiration from other artists is fine as long as you DO NOT COPY their work and claim it as your own. For my graduate thesis project, I had to create a series of work that was inspired by other artists. Inspiration could come from their style or their subject matter. But the final thesis product had to be my own creation, from start to finish. I had to document my own setups and photographs, color plans, materials, and finished work. All of this was part of the creative process.

I chose to do my work in two mediums: 12 oil paintings to match 12 hooked pieces.

I love hyperrealism and pop art. I was inspired by several modern artists like surrealist, René Magritte, and contemporary pop artists, like Wayne Thiebaud. For one project I combined the surrealism of Magritte by using the apple and scenery concept, but I added a candy apple in front of the face. My process was to first paint it, then hook it. You can see larger versions of these two pieces, shown below, on pages 100 and 101.

For me, the creative process is as important as the medium. The creative process will guide the project from start to finish and will ultimately determine the success of a project. Whether I am painting a portrait, a still life, or hooking a rug, my process is the same.

Process is important because it forces me to slow down and focus on the details rather than rush along. Process helps me analyze the project along the way and adjust as necessary. If I don't complete one of the process steps, it would be like a baker forgetting the baking powder in the cake, or forgetting to oil and flour a pan before pouring in the batter. For an artist, the creative process is the recipe one uses to make their art.

Often an art museum will highlight an artist process in a show. I have seen this approach with artists such as da Vinci and Rembrandt, and contemporary artists such Andrew Wyeth. Very few professional artists can "wing it." Having a process keeps an artist organized and focused on the project.

The creative process is a series of visual questions that you ask yourself as you begin.

- What inspired you to design this pattern?
- What is its ultimate purpose—is it a floor rug, wall hanging, or a gift?
- Which color do you want to dominate in the hooked piece?
- Do you want the background light, medium, or dark?
- Are you using as-is wool or hand dyed wool?
- Are there examples of this rug hooked by others you can refer to? Will you use special stitches or techniques to make sections stand out?
- How will you bind it?

Considering these questions before you begin will help you organize your thoughts and process. They will facilitate your planning and prevent burnout and frustration. Are you familiar with burnout? We have all experienced it. Burnout occurs when you have a project and suddenly, halfway through, you realize that you hate the colors you chose. Or the motif. Or the background you planned. I try to avoid burnout as much as possible.

Creating a Landscape Series

This is my process as I worked on a landscape series.

I start with a series of thumbnail sketches of the patterns I want to create. If I am doing a cohesive landscape series, I take a ton of photographs and edit them.

Sometimes I combine two photos into one. This allows me to use the background of one photo and add it into other photos to give the final image more interest.

In my photos, I am looking for specific things about the subject I am photographing. In this series, I wanted to place the palm trees against different backgrounds at different types of day. I wanted give them atmospheric perspective.

I then decide how I can emphasize the cohesiveness with a color or a style. In my coastal series, I used the same blues for the sky in each one, even though the foreground was different.

A gallery requested that I create 10 to 12 same-sized framed pieces. They wanted a "funky" style and a unique twist. And they wanted it to be a cohesive series. A cohesive series is a set of artworks that relates to each other. It enables collectors to choose pieces to add to their own personal collection. I created each piece with its own personality, and they all had their own names and identities. This helped me bring the images to life.

In this series I gave all of my palm trees the same-style trunks and placed them in different settings. I first took photos of palm trees at different times of the day and in different settings. I chose ten photos and drew sketches. I made colored-pencil studies and painted them in water-based gouache.

Then I lined up my painted pieces to make sure they worked in harmony. Once I was satisfied with the result, I drew out 8" squares on a large piece of monk's cloth. As I worked, I took photos of the individual piece in process, which allowed me to analyze my work and make adjustments as needed.

To finish, I covered each piece with a wet washcloth, steamed each, and waited until they dried. Then I cut them apart, adhering each piece to a separate backing to fit inside the frames. I could have framed the entire piece as one large hooking if I had planned to do that, as long as my hooking covered each outline and each square was the same size.

EVERYDAY CREATIVITY

As an artist, my creative process has become part of my daily routine. It gives me the foundation to continually feed my design ideas. You can do this too. A sketchbook is the perfect way to begin.

Collect photos and pictures that inspire you. Some day that photo, picture, scrap of cloth, or doodle will be the perfect spark for a project.

TIPS
for establishing your own creative process

1 Take lots of photos of everything that inspires you. Cut out images from magazines and catalogs that inspire you. Catalogs and magazines are great for color planning, too. The designers of the pages and ads know how to lay things out to make them attractive to the viewer.

2 Start a sketchbook and or journal. Make sketches daily.

3 Invest in a good set of colored pencils, markers, or other mark-making tools.

4 Document your color plans in your sketch book.

5 Follow other artists and rug makers on Pinterest and Instagram.

6 Subscribe to *Rug Hooking* magazine and ATHA for resources.

7 Join a local rug hooking group so you can work with other inspirational people, even if it is only virtual meetings.

8 Try different foundation materials in your work. Decide which one works best for you.

9 Try different techniques in your work. Experiment.

10 Set a time every day for rug hooking. Be consistent.

Creating with Children

One of the most rewarding aspects of rug hooking for me is teaching this textile art to others.

I enjoy teaching all ages of students—even children—and I find that I learn something from each student. When I have a table at an event or gallery show, I always have a piece of linen on the frame; I encourage people to try pulling a few loops through the foundation cloth to see if they might like to learn to hook.

In past years, prior to the pandemic, my summer art camp program took place inside for a weekly four-hour daily session. These included a 30-minute break. This gave me enough time to allow the children to design and hook their own patterns for a mat or pillow.

During this past summer of 2020, while we were in the midst of the COVID-19 pandemic, we had to improvise by designing a program that could accommodate the students while following the pandemic safety guidelines. Our camp took place for three weeks. We offered the camp in three one-week sessions, consisting of four days in the morning for two hours each day.

When I teach children, I ask the kids what they would like to do. I take their ideas and purchase clip art to inspire my designs for them. Children love bright colors and simple designs. There is a lot of inspiration in children's coloring books and sticker books.

When creating the kits for the kids in the camp, I follow the same process of designing as I do for adult work. I start with a concept sketch, then do a color study and draw out the pattern on linen. If I have time, I will hook the pattern ahead of time. But usually I want my young students to use their own creativity.

I place a box of wool strips on the table and let them pull out the colors they want. In this pandemic situation, I had to create pre-made kits, which meant choosing the colors ahead of time. The students rose to the occasion and used the colors they had in their kits. They also really enjoyed being outside in the nice weather while working and using their hands. The kids in my group all lived within a three-block area of each other and had "bubbled together" during this time. Their parents appreciated this creative time.

PART III
PROJECTS

Tile Rug

Creating depth and texture with wool

Tile Rug, *27" x 31", wool on linen. Designed and hooked by Victoria L. Rudolph, 2020. Outer border black-and-white squares and colored squares are 2". The remainder of the tiles are either 4" squares or 2" x 4" rectangles.*

The inspiration for Tile Rug *was the tile floor found in a doorway in San Luis Obispo, California. I appreciated the way the tile was laid in such a small space and the 2" black-and-white tiles in the border and 2" colored tiles throughout the space. The grout creates the illusion of different depths in the square and rectangular tiles.*

MATERIALS

- Photo or picture of tile template
- Sketch paper
- Colored pencils or paint
- Cardboard or plastic sheets to cut out your templates
- Scissors

- Construction pencil
- Foundation cloth of choice
- Yardstick and square templates
- Permanent markers
- Fabric pens

When I traveled to Barcelona in 2019, I was fascinated by the wonderful tiles used in the streets and walls in this Spanish city—especially the ones designed by Antoni Gaudí. I was especially drawn to the organic shapes and the geometrics. These tiles are a cultural design tradition in Barcelona.

Inspired by what I saw, I took hundreds of photographs and purchased a book of the designs. When I got home, I designed two of my favorite new rugs for my home. Now no matter where I go, I notice intricate tile patterns and photograph them for inspiration.

I like designing geometrics, or what I call tile rugs. A tile rug is a rug that has the same-size shape designed throughout the rug, and those fit together with smaller spacer tiles. I'll start with the rug design from San Luis Obispo.

The tiles in the original photograph were grouted to give the illusion of depth between the tiles. I imitated this by using a darker wool line around the square lines.

This is something you might find on a tiled floor or wall. Draw the shapes carefully and lay them out in a grid pattern. The pattern should feel harmonious. Then create a color plan on paper before you start to hook.

Even if you only have a few colors in your wool stash, you can still create a basic color plan. We tend to keep the wool colors we love. Work with these colors first. Can they work as a harmonious pattern when hooked together?

Whenever I plan a custom rug, I make two color plans, one for myself and one to give to my clients. As I lay out complicated patterns like tiles in a grid, sometimes I will have to resort to using a colored fabric marker to delineate the squares. (I know . . . earlier in these pages I said to never use color markers. But sometimes, just sometimes, I have to take the risk.)

There are times that I will have the design drawn out on paper and it looks perfect . . . until I lay it out on the foundation cloth. Seeing the design on the foundation might suggest a different configuration, so I have learned to adjust. In this project, I had to add colored markers (gasp!) to indicate where I would place each colored one-inch square.

I was careful to lay out the pattern on the foundation, but even with careful attention, I still had to adjust as I hooked.

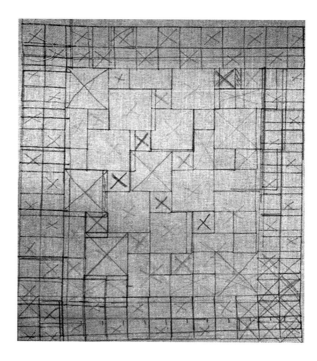

My "map" for hooking. Note the colored X's delineating the color plan.

Barcelona Tile Rug in Blue
Using shape and form to create patterns

Barcelona Tile Rug, *38" x 52", wool on linen. Designed and hooked by Victoria L. Rudolph, 2020.*

This rug was going to go in front of a bench in our bedroom. I wanted it to be large enough to fit the space but not so large that it might overwhelm the room. I was inspired by tiles in the *Barcelona Tile Book*. (The book grants permission to the reader to use images in the book for inspiration.) While not copying the exact pattern, I pulled two shapes together from different patterns and combined them with my own shapes to create my unique pattern.

Once I was happy with my rough sketch, I painted a color study in gouache water-based paints. I find that gouache colors match my dye colors the best, making it easier for me to see what the actual colors would be with my dyed wools.

Then I put the color plan next to my dyed wools to see if they would work. This is a huge help for me, allowing me to adjust and adapt and accurately predict how my rug will hook up.

I cut and serged my foundation cloth, and cut out templates to make my shapes.

A Note About Templates

Templates can be made from anything. It depends on the size you want for your rug. In this project, I used thin cardboard inserts I had saved from shirt and linen packaging. I have even saved the cardboard dividers from inside boxes of cat food tins.

I have also used plastic template paper and acrylic quilting templates that are available at most art supply and hobby stores. But for this project I had unusual shapes, so I had to make some of them from scratch. I kept the originals in case I wanted to hook this pattern again.

A template schematic for this rug is on page 105.

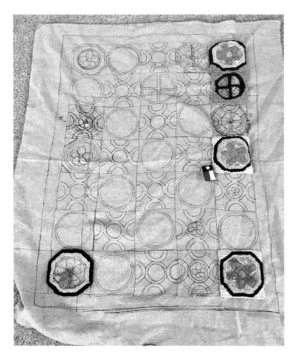

Then I starting hooking. I would stop after a few hours and leave it. When I returned later, I could more easily assess how it looked and determine if I liked it, if I was on the right track. When I felt comfortable with what I had done, I continued on hooking.

Playing with pattern design can be challenging but it is also rewarding. I spent several months designing this pattern by playing with the different shapes from photos and the inspiration that I drew from the *Barcelona Tile Book*. I narrowed it down to a few choice combinations that I liked. I discovered that by laying out the rug pattern first on paper and color planning it, I could visualize it already completed. Once I had the pattern transferred to the foundation cloth, I was able to hook it quickly.

Ancestral Family Clan Crest
Galbraith Family Clan Crest: "Ab Obice Suavier"

Translated from Latin, this motto is "Stronger when opposed."
Galbraith Clan Family Crest, *20" x 26", wool and wool plaid on linen. Designed and hooked by Victoria L. Rudolph, 2020.*
A celebration of ancestry and revival of Scottish customs. Anything can be used to inspire rug design.

MATERIALS

- JPEG or PDF image of crest (be sure to request permission, just to be on the safe side)

- Sketch paper

- Paint or colored pencils

- Foundation cloth

- Tracing paper or light box

- Construction pencil

- Permanent marker

- Scissors

- Serger

Many years ago, I discovered the extended history of my paternal grandfather's heritage. My paternal grandfather came from a long line of the Scottish Galbraith clan. "Galbraith" means "from Briton they came."

The Galbraiths had apparently supported and fought for the Saxon King William the Conquerer in 1066. As a reward for their loyalty and bravery, they were granted tracts of land in Fintry, Scotland, which lies between the highlands and the lowlands. No doubt William the Conquerer wanted loyal subjects representing him in Scotland and relied on this clan for information and business opportunities. The Galbraith clan built castles throughout the area.

The seventeenth chief was not good with finances and created a lot of conflicts with the British and Highlander authorities. He was forced to sell the castle to another clan. Many married into other clans or fled Scotland for the colonies or other countries around the world.

Today, the Galbraith family society are reunited through shared interest in our history, DNA, and reviving the customs of our Scottish ancestors. My Galbraith family is several thousand strong and each one of us is having DNA tests added to the databank. We may no longer have our castles in Scotland, but we are mighty and proud.

As a tribute to this part of my heritage, I decided to hook our family crest. I was granted permission from our family association board president to create this banner.

I took our logo to a reproduction shop and enlarged the design to my desired pattern size. I then created the color plan.

The painterly me painted the colors in gouache, water-based colors to match our logo requirements and to check the color plan.

Then, using my light box, I traced the pattern on to the drywall mesh and transferred it onto foundation cloth.

Current logo

My color plan

Ready to hook!

Luckily, I had enough wool in my stash that exactly matched the colors required by the Galbraith Family Society by-laws.

To make it even more authentic, I ordered 5/8" ribbon in our family tartan to edge the finished piece. Using the Doris Eaton finishing method I described on page 19, I used the tartan ribbon as my binding tape.

FACT

The Galbraith Family Society consists of 350 or more families around the world and are all connected by DNA. The mission of the group is to rekindle the history and spirit of our extended family. As a legally recognized group, we follow a specific structure, which demands a logo. We reworked our coat of arms using the Pantone Munsell system of colors.

Pantone Munsell System Colors

Pantone is a universal color guide system, recognized and used by creative professionals. This system creates the standard for colors. Pantone uses the Munsell system of colors in their process. Every professional creative has used a form of the Pantone color system. I guaranteed that anytime you see a brand logo with color, the logo was developed using this system.

Pantone Munsell System (PMS) is the system of colors used in graphic design, textiles, and for coatings and pigments. It is used by every industry that uses color in their business. Pantone even establishes the color trends for each year.

As a young artist I marveled over the chip books I found at work. I think this is what drove me to become an artist and study color theory.

In the Galbraith Clan rug, my task was to match the dyed colors to the PMS colors the family had chosen for their coat of arms. I knew I could match the color. Knowing how to use this system helped me facilitate my dye process too. Pantone Munsell also has other systems for textiles called TCX and TPG for pigments and coatings. But all of these colors systems work in the same way.

I invested in a Pantone color chip system to help me design my rug projects and paintings. I am also always grateful when a client asks for a specific color in the PMS system.

For more information about this system visit www.Pantone.com.

Creating a Series on One Piece of Foundation Cloth

MATERIALS

- Foundation cloth

- Permanent markers

- Rulers

- Square or rectangular templates

- Frames

I sell a lot of my work through galleries. Most require a cohesive series. This means they want a body of work of the same size and related to the same theme.

I enjoy hooking these sets of the same size. I often hook them together on one piece of foundation cloth so I can see my progress along the way. It helps me to view the pieces as part of a set and imagine how they will appear framed. It also helps me to decide how to put them into an order once they are completed and framed. It encourages critical comparison and helps me edit as the series evolves.

Some rug hookers draw up several items like Christmas stockings, ornaments, and pillows on one piece of foundation cloth. It saves both time and money. I often design my kits in the same way. I minimize wastage on foundation cloth.

Inspired by my time living on the coast, seeing the ocean and landscape change with the tides, I created several coastal landscape scenes by taking photographs in my hometown. I reviewed the photos, and enlarged or cropped them to the final size I wanted to hook.

Complete series, not yet framed

If using this method, first sketch out your proposed series on paper. Choose or create the appropriate-shaped template; enlarge it to the desired finished size so that the series will fit on your foundation. This also helps you determine how much room you will have between the rows for finishing. I recommend this method if you hook on a rug hooking frame. If you use a hoop instead, it is more challenging to hook multiple pieces, as the thickness of one hooked portion may make it hard to fit the rest of the foundation cloth into the hoop.

For this series, I used custom float frames. Float frames have a deeper setback for the artwork, which makes the art appear to float and gives the finished piece a three-dimensional feel. Float frames come in many sizes; I order multiples in advance to make sure each frame is exactly the same size and color for my cohesive series. It is important that my pieces fit snugly into the frame for the overall effect.

When deciding how many smaller bits you want to

hook on one piece of cloth, figure out your actual finished size first. This will determine how large your foundation cloth must be. I apply the following formula to determine the final size of the foundation cloth: If using 6", 7", or 12" squares, add 6" to the top and sides so you have enough overage as you hook the end squares. Then add 4" between the rows so you have enough room to have a 2" finish seam. Lay out the designs and add the total number of inches per row, including the ends, which are 6". Do this both vertically and horizontally; the totals will give you the dimensions of foundation cloth required.

Whether creating series for a gallery or for beginner kits, I always use this same formula. This also ensures that all the pieces on the pattern are the correct size. I order gallery frames in bulk so that they will always be the same size and color.

Sometimes I have a piece of odd-sized linen. I will measure it out and, if possible, hook more squares. Even if your lines between the rows aren't perfect, as long as the squares are the same size and you have enough seam allowance, it will work.

Float frame

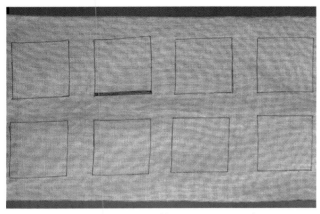

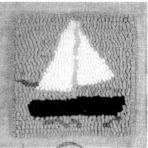

Sailboat packaged kit

Linen with boxes (showing correction)

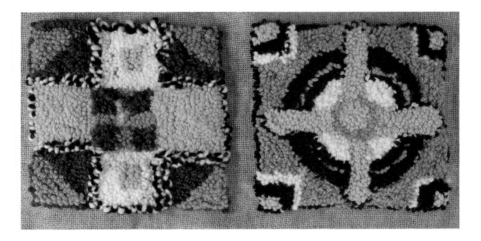

Needle punch

I often make kits for my Etsy site and my classes. I usually end up with several orders for the same patterns, so it is easy to create several squares at once. Then when I receive an order, I can easily pull the pattern and pair it with the wool to create a kit.

Hooked kit samples

Christmas Tree Skirt

Phyllis Harrelson's Christmas Tree Skirt

Harrelson Christmas Tree Skirt, *48" round, wool on linen with cotton backing. Designed by Victoria L. Rudolph and hooked by Phyllis Harrelson.*

MATERIALS

- Circle template

- Permanent marker

- Foundation cloth, 75/76" wide

- Pattern designs for each wedge

Years ago, one of my students and dear friend Phyllis came to me and wanted to create a Christmas tree skirt. We measured the size and circumference of a tree skirt she had and then drew up a pattern. In this photo, I added a small amount to each side to make sure there was enough space for cutting around the circle.

She backed it with fabric.

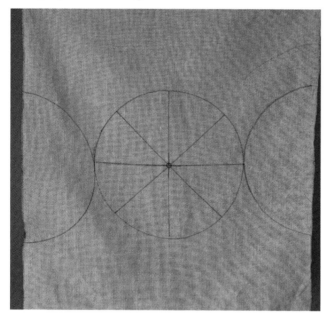

After a few edits on the designs, we took the pattern and had it enlarged at a copy shop to the desired size. We cut out the pattern and pinned it to the linen.

I use drywall crack mesh to make my patterns because I can use them over and over and they stick to the linen. Here it is in progress.

Ready to celebrate Christmas!

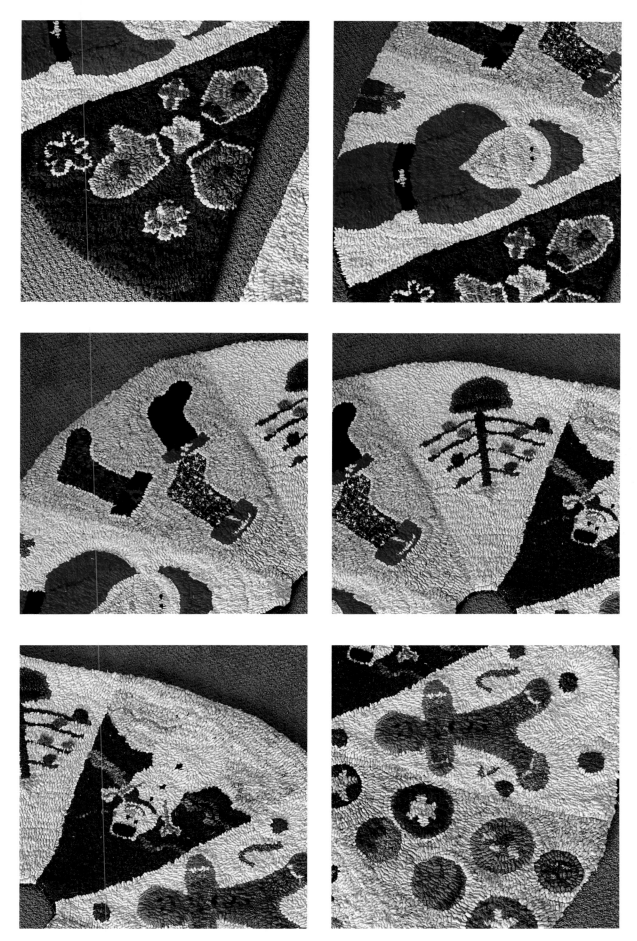

Hooked Vest

MATERIALS

- Foundation cloth of choice, either linen or monk's cloth

- Vest pattern

- Pins

- Black permanent markers

- Scissors

- Fabric for back of vest

- Templates if needed for pattern to be hooked on vest

- Needle and thread or sewing machine

Sometimes I'm inspired to create an unusual hooked piece. Inspiration might be an art contest or something in my local environment. When we lived in Denver a few years ago, I taught rug hooking to adults and children at a students' art league. All the instructors were invited to participate in a wearable art show.

I decided to make a vest. I purchased a simple vest pattern and then cut out the pattern and pinned it onto the linen foundation cloth that I would hook into. I wanted a dark background and bright pennies. I would add sari silk ribbon as a wavy stripe between the pennies. All these materials, plus the matching yarn for a whipstitch finished edge, were already in my stash. I purchased ultrasuede (for the back) and satin (for the lining) in the same colors. Both sides of the vest were hooked at the same time on one piece of linen.

If you want to hook a similar vest, I recommend these steps:

1. Pick a simple vest pattern.
2. Transfer the pattern to the linen. Laying out clothing patterns on linen is similar to laying out a hooking design for a rug or pillow.
3. Prepare a piece of foundation cloth that is a large square or rectangle. Secure the edges by either serging, sewing, or taping. Cut out your chosen pattern. Confirm that you have all the pieces you need for the entire completed piece.

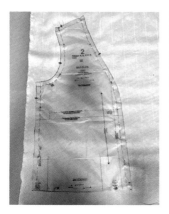 

4. Pin down the front side pattern (right or left) of the vest to the linen. Sewing pattern pieces are drawn to include a seam allowance, but for this project you should add a 2" border beyond the pattern, between the two vest sides. Repeat this process with the opposite front piece. You can do this on one large piece of linen as long as you include at least a 2" border separating the two pieces of linen. Trace the edges of the pattern with a permanent marker. Remove the paper pattern and draw in the seam allowance. I put a pin on the seam allowance line so I am sure it is correct before I draw it in.
5. Repeat this with the right side of the vest pattern. Don't draw beyond the seam allowance. Trace the seam allowance on the foundation cloth.

6. Do the same with the vest backing pattern. For the vest back, I used an ultrasuede with a satin lining, but you can also use any durable cloth that will wear well. Here I show it with the back-pattern piece on the monk's cloth because it was easier to photograph the process.
   a.) Fold the back fabric in half.
   b.) Trace around the pattern with a permanent marker.
   c.) Cut the pattern without cutting the fold. This will give you the entire back so you don't need to seam it.

7. It is time to hook! I hooked the entire front panels, which results in a heavier finished vest, but I wanted my vest to have a completely hooked front.

"I wear this vest often and always get compliments. This is a great way to show off your passion for rug hooking."

Mermaid
Three-dimensional whimsy

Hooked mermaid tail

MATERIALS

- Monk's cloth or linen

- #3-cut wool strips in multiple colors

- Permanent marker

- Template paper: plastic template paper, cardboard, or freezer paper

- Needle and thread

- Wire

- Embroidery needle

- Embroidery thread in the colors of the mermaid's tail

- Polyfil for stuffing the body and tail

- Scissors

- Serger or tape

- Fabric markers (optional)

When I moved to the coast, I wanted to make a sculpture of a mermaid for every coastal community near me. Each one would have a name representing her location and her relationship to the sea and her mermaid legends. This series is still a work in progress.

There will be a total of six mermaids, honoring our favorite Pacific Coastal communities. The first mermaid is named Hali Magan Bijou. The first two words in her name are Greek, meaning "sea" and "pearl" respectively; her last name is the French word for "pearl."

Other mermaids will be named Oceana (meaning "from the sea") for Ocean Beach in San Francisco; Pasha (meaning "ocean") for Pacifica; Shasa (meaning "precious water") for Santa Cruz; Maeve (Irish meaning "goddess of song") for Monterey; and finally, Avila (one of our favorite beaches in San Luis Obispo).

This project afforded me valuable lessons in three-dimensional construction. This project combined doll making, embroidery, and rug hooking. The trial-and-error process brought this mermaid to life and was well worth the time and effort.

Don't be afraid to experiment with an idea and make mistakes. Sometimes the mistakes end up becoming part of the identity and personality of the piece.

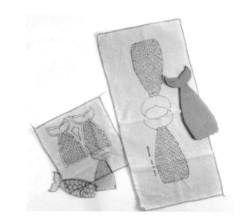

Mermaid pattern

Mermaid tail scales

I wanted the sculpture to be about 16" long, sitting on a dowel of about 9". I consider hooking this on linen, but I realized it would be harder to manipulate the body into the shape I wanted, so I used monk's cloth.

I created a doll pattern for the head and upper bodice. Or consider using a premade soft doll form. It doesn't really matter which doll pattern you use as long as you make the tail pattern large enough to fit around the torso. The patterns included are for both a 9" and 16" mermaid tail.

1. Copy the template to the size you desire onto the template paper. Notice the tail is connected at the end. This is to allow you to fold the tail over and sew the sides to the upper body. (If you use a premade cloth doll's body with wire, you can sew the inside of the legs together before you insert it into the hooked outer tail.) For my example, I made just the upper torso, added the wire into the body, and sewed the bottom piece. Then I attached the hooked tail to the upper torso. I also embroidered her eyes and tattoos. I used sari silk for her top.
2. Trace the template onto monk's cloth. With a marker, add a 1½" seam allowance on each side, all around the tail pattern.
3. Treat the edges of the foundation cloth so it doesn't fray. I usually serge the edges, but you can sew or tape them.
4. Hook both sides of the tail pattern.
5. Cut out the tail with enough room to fold in the edges, and then carefully fold the tail in half so that the right sides of the hooked areas are facing each other.
6. Place this around the doll's body to measure the linen you want to sew together. Then very carefully cut out the center of the area between the fins. Do NOT cut the two fin sets apart.
7. Sew the seam on the open side so that the hooking meets neatly around the tail fin and up one side.
8. Turn right side out and fit to the doll's upper body.
9. Stuff the inside of the tail all the way down to the fin. Make sure it isn't so fat that it won't fit around the bodice.
10. Tuck the last sides in, and carefully sew up the side. Attach to the bodice with a whip stitch with either thread or matching embroidery floss.

Cetus Balena (The Whale)
More seaside whimsy

MATERIALS

- Monk's cloth or linen

- Hook

- Scissors

- Template paper or cardboard

- Ruler

- Permanent marker

- Small hollow tube to fit the dowel or rebar

- Needle

- Thread

- Permanent glue

- Base and dowel: in this case, rebar and ceramic half-dome piece

- Stuffing

By now you can see that inspiration for my projects comes directly from the environment I inhabit. The first week I arrived in Half Moon Bay, California, I saw whales, dolphins, and seals swimming along our coast. It was awe-inspiring. The whales were migrating south towards Mexico from Alaska. Sea birds flew above them as they followed the whales, watching for fish.

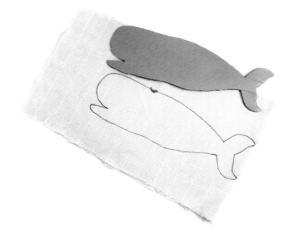

I lived in the Colorado mountains prior to moving to the coast, and I was reminded of the many varieties of wildlife I have been fortunate to encounter. Each place I have visited or lived provided me inspiration for my art, but nothing compared to the mighty Pacific Ocean.

I had seen many wooden, metal, and ceramic sculptures of whales, but I could not find a single one made of fiber. I wanted something for my house that was meaningful and thus decided to create this whale.

For most of projects for this book, I dyed my own wool. For this whale sculpture, I used spot dyes and my favorite shade of my own pink recipe for the background.

Begin by drawing your pattern on the foundation cloth; I used monk's cloth. It is easy to fold. I first laid the template against the folded edge and drew it on. Then I unfolded the monk's cloth and traced the template so that the tail edge matched exactly. I wanted the tails to be the point at which these two sides connected. I added 1½" of border all around the pattern for the seam allowance.

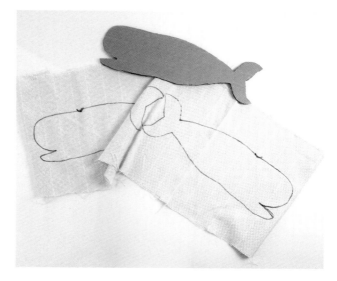

I hooked one side, then folded the foundation cloth to make sure they were still even. Then I hooked the other side. I added proddy flowers to embellish.

Once the hooking was completed, I very carefully cut away the foundation cloth, leaving space around the tail; I added a liquid adhesive so that the edges would not fray. When this dried, I folded over the bottom edges of the tail and sewed the bottom of the tail together.

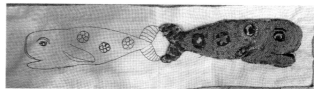

Next I sewed the whale body together, except for the mouth area, also leaving a small gap on the top for a blow spout and a small hole at the bottom center for the mounting stick or post.

I used the open mouth to stuff the whale, then sewed up the mouth. I embellished a strip of wool with metallic thread and beads to stiffen it, then added two strips of metallic ribbon to the front and back of this for the spout water.

To mount this whale, I purchased a rebar stand and ceramic half dome from my ceramist friend and teacher Judy Vassar. You can easily use any solid base and a wooden dowel to mount a sculpture like this. (Rebar is a steel rod used in commercial construction and can be found at home building supply stores.) I glued the half dome ceramic piece to the base and filled the interior of the base with a foam filler. Once this dried, I inserted a small open tube into the bottom of my whale to fit snugly around the top of the rebar stand, holding my whale in place.

This was one of my favorite projects.

Embellished Bags
Show off your art on market day

MATERIALS

- Linen: enough to construct a cloth market bag

- Or use an existing cloth bag

- Scissors

- Needle and thread

- Embroidery thread

- Template

- Plastic interfacing

- Fusible iron adhesive

- Handles, cotton duck (optional)

I always get compliments when I carry these bags. They are not heavy, and I use them for library trips and light shopping. They also make great teacher, hostess, and birthday gifts.

Sometimes I will be commissioned to create a kit specifically for a class. I normally paint the design first and create a color plan ahead of time. One school on the coast wanted a sunset theme. I showed them several photographs of sunsets I had taken during my evening strolls. They chose the one shown on page 68 and asked me to teach how to sew it onto the bag too. I was able to match the sunset colors with the wool.

I create and sell kits, and I am always at a loss as to where to display my samples. I purchased a few linen bags and realized it would be fun to sew my samples on the front of these bags. But even if you didn't have such a bag, you could easily create it from either linen or monk's cloth.

Getting ready to make the bags:
1. Cut the piece of linen to 32" x 32".
2. Serge the edges.
3. Create a template for the pattern: square, rectangular, or circular.

Option 1: Use an existing bag

When I finish my kit samples, I sew them to the front of the linen bags I purchased. This is a very simple process. Take the hooked piece and make sure the raw edges are folded to the back and sewn down. Using the entire six threads of matching embroidery floss, sew the pattern to the bag with a whip stitch. Weave the end of your thread through the bottom and back of the whip stitch.

Cut a piece of fusible interfacing the same size as the hooked piece. Turn the bag inside out; iron the fusing to the back side of the hooking. Turn your bag right side out and it is completed.

Because you are using a linen bag, you can also hook a border right into the bag around the pattern. Or, get creative and use your imagination: invent other ways to embellish your bag.

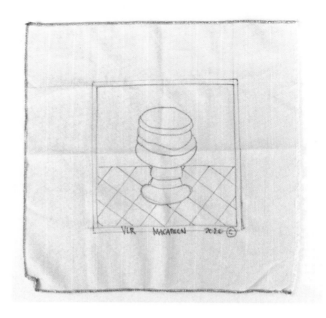

Macaroon ready to hook

Macaroon bag

Skull bag

Option 2: Sew your own bag

Plan the size of your bag and cut a piece of linen double that size, remembering to include room for seams. Fold the linen in half and transfer the pattern onto the front of one side. Make sure it is centered in the middle of the linen.

Hook your bag. Measure out and cut a piece of iron-on interfacing to fit over your hooked design. It should be large enough to cover the entire size of the design. Turn the fabric to the wrong side (back side of the hooked pattern). Iron the interfacing onto the back side of the hooked area. Draw a ¼" seam along the side of the bag and sew up to the top. Repeat on the other side, then fold the top edge of the bag to the inside and sew down to finish the top edge. Add handles if you wish. I use a durable duck cotton for handles.

Colorado bag

Heart bag

My Secret Garden
Get creative! Three-dimensional hooked and embroidered creation

My Secret Garden, *12" in 6-paneled hexagon box; wool, yarn, cotton floss, sari silk ribbon, wool roving, pipe cleaners, and beads on monk's cloth. Designed and hooked by Victoria L Rudolph, 2020.*

MATERIALS

- Any size box

- Pencil/colored pencils

- Eraser

- Graph paper

- Foundation cloth

- Cut wool strips in desired size for interior and exterior walls, coils, and flowers

- Yarn, sari silk ribbon

- Embroidery floss

- Glass beads

- Pipe cleaners

- Wool roving for needle felting

- Heavy-duty double stick adhesive

My husband and I love to visit botanical gardens. I am fascinated with the way these gardens are planned and cultivated.

Gardens are great to recreate with hooking and textiles. Inspired by the book *Embroidered Knot Gardens*, by Owen Davies, of the Royal School of Needlework, UK, and having taken many classes in embroidery and needle felting over the years, I decided that a hooked garden would be a fun project. Always looking for a new idea or challenge for my artwork, I decided to create my own three-dimensional gardens. I recreated favorite elements from the gardens I visited, such as topiaries, fountains, wall boxes, and sculpture.

My first one was in a tiny green box that had hinges and a glass top. Using graph paper, I sketched out the dimensions of the interior size of the box and transferred this pattern onto foundation cloth. I hooked the garden hedges with both spotted green and a solid green textured wool in a #8 cut. Then I filled in the flowers using warm, bright colors of red, orange, yellow, and pink. A walking path was one piece of white textured wool. A fountain was constructed with stacked blue wool coils and beads.

The combination of warm flowers surrounding the cool fountain worked nicely together. I created several prototypes and each time added something new. Finally, I decided that I wanted to create the whole garden, including the exterior and interior walls.

For this secret garden, I used a hexagon box I purchased from a hobby store. You can use any box you desire, but hinged boxes don't really allow for adding interior or exterior hooked walls, so you will have to sand, prime, and paint the hinged boxes.

Reverse hooking brick pattern

THE MAIN GARDEN

1. Trace the bottom of your box onto paper.
2. Place the paper into your box to see how it fits. Trim as necessary to fit snugly. This will be the base of your garden.
3. Measure the walls of your box. Using the exact measurements, draw this on paper or measure exactly on your foundation cloth, making sure all your walls are on the same line of the foundation cloth and evenly spaced (see photo, page 74). Add a ¼" seam allowance between each wall block so when you wrap the hooked foundation cloth around your box, the corners will fit nicely. Add a 2" seam allowance to the top and the bottom of the wall block strips. This will be sewn and folded prior to attachment. Once you have drawn the lines on your foundation cloth for the walls, place this on the box as you hook to check your measurements.
4. This is the time to add doors or trees or anything else you want to include. You will simply hook the brick wall around these elements.
5. You can hook any way that you want. I used a reverse brick hooking pattern from Ingrid Hieronimus's book, *Special Effects Using Creative Stitches*. This is a wonderful resource for learning unique stitches for rug hooking.
6. When completed, steam your work with a wet cloth and let dry.
7. Add external or internal wall elements that need to be embroidered, such as vines and flowers.
8. Cut the exterior and interior wall strips, sew the seam allowance down, and steam.

THE FOUNTAIN

1. Decide the size of your fountain.
2. Cut out a circle of blue wool to serve as the base. Appliqué this to the foundation cloth in the location where you will add the actual fountain.
3. Make several wool coils in the colors of your choice in graduating sizes to create a stacked wedding cake. Feel free to embellish them as you desire.
4. Sew the coils together and add beaded strings around the fountain structure. You can also add sparkling items like iridescent pipe cleaners. Set this aside until you have completely hooked the garden.

PUTTING IT ALL TOGETHER:

1. Glue the exterior wall panel onto the outside of the box. Repeat for the interior walls.
2. Whipstitch the top of the panels together with a strong neutral yarn. I used white to match the corners of the box, which is raw foundation cloth.
3. Add the elements to the base of the garden. I created a pipe cleaner sculpture, felted topiaries, and a fountain. Sew these to the base with matching thread. Use whatever method works to attach these items.
4. Carefully place this base into the box. You might have to adjust the inside walls a bit; if you measured correctly it should fit snugly.

The interior of My Secret Garden, *showing some of the three-dimensional structures*

GAL

m

A RUG HOOKED CO

LERY

LECTION OF SWEETS

Working in Multiple Mediums

It doesn't matter what style of art is your preferred medium; anything you can create in one medium can be easily transferred to rug hooking.

In graduate school, I was required to focus on one of the foundational fine arts (painting, sculpture, or drawing). Most of my graduate school courses involved learning to refine my skills according to the foundational rules of fine art—the characteristics of shape, shadow, and color. As a result, I learned a new way of seeing and speaking about these.

When it was time to declare my thesis, I proposed submitting my final work in two mediums. I wanted to demonstrate that these acquired and honed foundational skills could translate easily to rug hooking. This was a departure from the typical graduate thesis project, but the school was intrigued by the possibilities.

The requirements from the department head were three:

1. I had to present a cohesive theme.
2. My rug hookings needed to contain the same values as the paintings.
3. The subjects would be my own setups and derived from my own photographs.

Those requirements were easy. I would use oil paintings as my color studies for the rug hookings. I began to plan my work with these requirements in mind.

It honestly didn't matter if I used landscape, still life, or portrait as my subject matter—I knew they would all translate into wool. The concepts of shape, shadow, and color helped me organize my projects ahead of time. My subject of choice? Baked goods and sweets!

Once I determined my cohesive theme, I was required to create 12 pairs of paintings and matching rugs. I only had 18 months to complete the thesis. I planned on finishing two paintings and two rugs per 15-week semester.

Each project for this thesis was a valuable learning experience. I had to submit sketches, photograph setups, progress photos, and written descriptions describing my work and the process. Then I would adjust the pieces according to the professor's recommendations and resubmit each piece for approval. This was time consuming, but it enabled each student to be successful at completing the requirements for graduation. The feedback from these sessions was priceless. It taught me to slow down, think a project through from start to finish, and problem solve. It gave me time to reflect on each piece and each step: subject setup, pattern design, color planning, and finishing.

This gallery will show you some of my painting-transformed-into-wool pairings.

Creating in two mediums is time consuming but it is a whole lot of fun too. This series was created over a short period of time, so each piece was allotted a specific amount of time for production. Looking back, I wish I had more time to make more adjustments — but the time constraints forced me to keep going. Overall, my project was hugely successful.

Whatever lesson I learned from one project was applied in another. The most rewarding result was to see the hooked pieces evolve from the painted pieces and original photographs. My photographs were created from my own setups of these objects and were for reference only. Technically, one could say this series was done in three mediums, because the photographs had to be lighted in such a way that I could see all the shapes in light and shadow. In the end, I had a cohesive body of work and learned valuable lessons in the process.

It is absolutely NOT necessary to create a cohesive series of work to become a better rug hooker. Nor it is necessary to be a trained artist. The joy of rug hooking is claiming it for yourself and hooking according to your own style.

My first piece was called *Macaroons!* After sketching out this idea, I took a photograph of a plate of macaroons. I knew that too many colors of macaroons would be distracting for the viewer. Instead, I chose a complimentary color palette of purple and yellow. Each macaroon had to be designed to carry the weight of several values (from light to dark) of both the colors to distinguish one from the other.

The painting was a little bit more tinted than the final piece, but it worked. The darkest side of each macaroon as a whole could not be as light as the lightest side. Each piece had to be divided into separate forms of light and dark. To create an edge for each macaroon, I needed a different value distinct from the value I used on the side of the macaroon.

I was trying to create a puzzle from scratch. I used eight values of each of the yellow and the purple colors. This macaroon hooking would be the largest of the collection.

To save time, I dyed the yellows myself and sourced the purples elsewhere. I also had to dye a subtle, muted mixture of the yellow and the purple to act as a "bridge color" between the two. I coordinated with the person who dyed the purple for me; I asked her which formulas she used so I could use the same in order to be able to achieve a better blend.

While the end result was successful, my piece was way too large and I used way too much of my budgeted time. In this semester, I was only able to complete one piece with its matching painting. Nevertheless, I really enjoyed seeing this project come to life.

Macaroons!
Oil on canvas panel, 14" x 11", 2016

Macaroons!
Wool on linen, 33" x 39", 2016

Inspired by artist Wayne Thiebaud, I wanted to create a painting and rug that had a soft but realistic quality. Theibaud started his art career as an illustrator and brought these skills to his paintings. His work spanned several art movements, but he is also known for his pop-art paintings of everyday items. The subjects he painted were recognizable and enticing. That is what I wanted to achieve in both the painting and rug hooked piece. Theibaud is my favorite pop artist painter and I love his color palette.

I photographed three different flavors of macaroons with a warm light, then mixed my oil colors from scratch, which helped to narrate the texture. The hooked piece was much more challenging because I wanted a cooler palette. I also changed the chocolate macaroon in the back to a raspberry one because I couldn't dye my wool the appropriate browns to work well. (The values remained the same.) I used dotted wool to create the air holes found in the macaroon cookies.

I also used a brighter, lighter white, which I dyed mottled gray, to emphasize the light I captured in the painting.

Trois Macaroon
Oil on canvas panel, 18" x 14", 2016

Trois Macaroon
Wool on linen, 24" x 36", 2016

This series that I created for my graduate thesis project was inspired by my fond childhood memories of a love for sweets and baked goods as well as my love for pop art. And, as an artist, I am obsessed with color, shape, texture, and pattern. As I progressed in creating this series, I applied the lessons and techniques I learned from each pairing. Those lessons helped me create each new pair of painting and hooking. Each pair built upon the others.

In *Cupcake and Lolly*, I truly enjoyed experimenting with the different elements. I gathered a painted tin plate, a giant cupcake that I commissioned from a a baker friend, and a jumbo swirled lollypop. Of course, it had my signature bright color palette! I created the layout and took many photos of this project before I began.

Once I settled on the layout, it was full steam ahead. My friend baked the cupcake and decorated it with fondant in colors that matched the lollypop. She covered the cupcake in fondant and filled it underneath with a lot of icing to hold up the fondant. Then she added some matching candy on top. I used several values of each color to recreate the depth and dimensions. I wanted to also capture the gloss on the lollypop and the textured feel of the checkered plate. My studio walls at the time were painted a bright pink, which allowed me to take advantage of shadows when photographing setups. Once again, I used many values of each color to recreate this in wool. The gloss on the lollypop was the hardest to recreate. I used sparkly wool to help build the glossy effect on the lollypop. Today I might use a sari silk to help with this effect.

The shadow in the rug was a lot darker than in the painting, so I added more shadow on the darker edge of the cupcake in the hooked piece. The plate came out really well. I used different dyed blacks that had other colors to imitate the plate.

Cupcake & Lolly
Oil on canvas panel, 14" x 11", 2016

Cupcake & Lolly
Wool on linen, 24" x 18", 2016

Sometimes it is so easy to translate a painting to a hooked piece that is almost difficult to tell one apart from the other.

I bought a decorated box of cupcakes, photographed them in the box, then cropped my photo. I wanted to focus on just the cupcakes and their dimensions. The box was clear, with tones of blue that showed up well when photographed, which made it easier to hook the edges. Recreating the decorations and icing was the most interesting part of this project. Here I used lots of different values of each of the cupcake colors in wool to create a sense of depth and shape.

Cupcakes in a Box
Oil on canvas, 12" x 9", 2016

Cupcakes in a Box
Wool on linen, 18" x 24", 2016

During the time I was working on my thesis, my dear friend Joey Kay and her sister were on a trip to Hong Kong and stopped at a pastry shop. She knew I was doing this project and offered to help with the subject matter. She sent me a photo that her sister took of her holding a half-eaten cupcake.

The wonderful thing about this photo was that there was a three-dimensional quality to it. The cupcake and hand were foreshortened. This means they are larger than the rest of the image and up front on the ground plane. The rest of her body was in dark clothing and there was a glass door with landscaping behind her. It was a great design to paint and hook.

The challenge with this project was creating shading, the thumb, and the nail polish. I used several shades of red to recreate the nail polish, the icing, and the cherry. The cupcake had air bubbles and bits of dried fruit, so that was easy to create. Because the landscape was in the background, I only needed to create the illusion of the door and greenery behind it. It was light enough against the sweater to create the illusion of depth. The most challenging section was separating the thumb from the napkin underneath.

This is one of my favorite pieces of the series. It is unique and fun.

Joey's Cupcake
Oil on canvas panel, 14" x 11", 2016

Joey's Cupcake
Wool on linen, 20" x 16", 2016

When researching the baked goods and sweets topic, I had a fabulous time going to several bakeries and confectioners. My favorite baker was known for themed cakes. This display was sitting in her shop and she was excited for me to use it for the project. About the time I started this series, French macaroons and mini-cupcakes were popular embellishments for cakes.

I took a ton of photos. This was my most technically challenging project. It contained a lot of different elements, each with its own shapes and shadows. The icing was a buttercream, with purple and pink macaroons and decorated mini-cupcakes and cookies on top. I added pearl beads to the top to imitate the candy pearls. Even the little candy pearls had shadows. the cupcake in the front cast a shadow down the front of the cake. The macaroon cast shadows.

I created a striped background because the cake was placed against a beige wall in the bakery, and this didn't work well on the canvas. The cake plate was soft white porcelain and difficult to recreate. I should have used cooler grays in the base instead of the warmer grays I did use. I had to redo this part several times.

I chose a spotted wool in greens to differentiate the background wall from the foreground, with subtle light on the right side. In retrospect, I forgot the cast shadow facing towards the wall and the gradual darkening from left to right in the stripes, but elements came out better than I could have imagined. My professor suggested I included a transition between the background and the foreground, which is why I have the "molding" line between the background and the tabletop. I used a beading method on this part. I will probably redo this one again someday to see if I can improve on it.

Macaroon Wedding Cake
Oil on canvas panel, 24" x 18", 2016

Macaroon Wedding Cake
Wool on linen, 24" x 18", 2016

Since I was a child, I have loved red candy apples. Every fall my family would enjoy these treats and they became a tradition. I love the feel and look of the glossy candy and how it cracks, and the cinnamon taste when you bite into it. When I was researching subjects for this project, I knew I would include these in the series.

I placed the candy apples on a bright white quartz surface and lit the wall behind it. The painting came out exactly as I wanted. I enjoyed hooking this piece. I thought it translated well from the painting to the wool.

Translating these values to the wool was a little challenging because wool tends to soften the image. Each apple took the light differently, and I had to use several values of red and some greens to make them appear three-dimensional. I used wool that I already had in my stash and also dyed some wool for the darker spots of the apples. I added some green to the dye pot.

In the end I think I should have used a darker line between the ground plane and the background, but overall, the hooked piece worked.

Candy Apples
Oil on canvas panel, 9" x 12", 2016

Candy Apples
Wool on linen, 18" x 24", 2016

I love color and I love pop art. My palette tends to be bright hues, though I enjoy all colors. I found these tin containers in the candy aisle around Valentine's Day and couldn't resist buying all the colors. When doing this series, I had to pay homage to this brand of candy and its pop art quality.

I call M&M's brand the Crayola of the candy world because they have so many colors. They have branded this candy and it has taken a life of its own. It has its own shops, merchandise, and every year new flavors and colors. You can even arrange to purchase monogrammed candies for special occasions.

The colors I used here are true to the actual tins. I placed them according to a color wheel and I sourced or dyed matching colors to use in this hooked rug. The light source came from above, but it was lightest in the middle and out to the left. Each M&M has several values. I tea-dyed the wool background for the darker parts of the rug.

M & M's in a Color Wheel
Oil on canvas panel, 36" x 24", 2016

M & M's in a Color Wheel
Wool on linen, 33" x 39", 2016

Donut Study
Oil on canvas, 9" x 12", 2015

In *Donut Study*, I was attracted to the colors and textures of the donuts, and I marveled at the icing and decorations on top. When I first saw these donuts, they were displayed in an elevated standing and rotating glass shelf. The donut shop did this deliberately to entice their customers to purchase more.

I bought them (the beautiful display worked on me!) and decided to photograph the donuts from above to keep the eye moving around the canvas. I changed the layout on the rug pattern slightly to show more of the donuts.

My largest challenge with this piece was how to recreate the sprinkles on top. I settled on glass beads. I had never used beading in my rug hooking before, but since this piece would be hung on a wall rather than on the floor, I decided it was worth a try. Since then, I have been using beads and other items frequently in my hooked pieces.

In this project I dyed wool to match the donut colors. Each of those colors have different values to help create the illusion of the donut shape. I made sure the donut holes were visible.

The moral of this project is this: Don't be afraid to experiment with other materials when creating your hooked pieces. In the end, while I like the painting, I think the rug was more successful because the sprinkles look realistic in the hooked piece. The donuts look real. I would have used a real piece of bubble gum but I was worried about moths being attracted to the rug.

There are no rules about creating backgrounds. In this hooking, I felt it was important to create movement in a piece where the motifs were so similar in color to the background wool. While I added a cast shadow under each donut, I wanted the background to separate itself as an object.

My goal was to create a surface under the donuts like pastry paper and to enhance the illusion of a three-dimensional shape. I accomplished this by outlining the donuts with the background wool and extending the lines in many directions. I also subtly variegated the background wool. I chose background wool pieces in colors and values that were very similar. This added a little more interest to such a large area of "negative space."

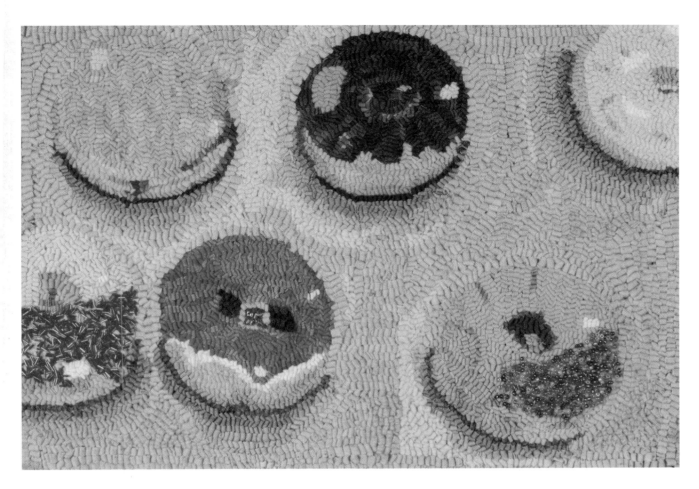

Donut Study
Wool and glass beads on linen, 18" x 24", 2015

TIP

Negative space is the area around your objects, the area that forms the background. It is important to address this space too. I see negative space as the "bridge" to the rest of the objects. It needs to have its own life. There are times when a straight hooked background serves the piece better, but that is not always the case. You can make the background an integral part of the design itself.

I discovered this larger 5" macaroon late one afternoon. It was sitting alone in the bakery display case on a gold-foiled paper tray on a reflective metallic glass pedestal. I loved how the light bounced off of it.

But the view behind it was boring. Once again, I added stripes. I had this wonderful black and white reverse polka-dotted wool that would make a wonderful striped background, especially if I hooked both sides. I painted it vertically but ended up hooking it horizontally, which in the end I preferred.

I used different values of gold on the left side to show the gold reflections. The filling was piped cream between raspberries, and tightly packed. In my hooked piece, the raspberry and cream becomes darker as it recedes to the far right.

Macaroon Tart on a Pedestal
Oil on canvas panel, 12" x 9", 2016

Macaroon Tart on a Pedestal
Wool on linen, 18" x 24", 2016

Kseni Bakery Display
Oil on canvas, 24" x 18", 2016

Inspiration for my rug designs comes from many places. I keep a clip-art inspirational journal of images and colors that attract me, and I find that I refer to my journal when designing. I have these books filled with magazine ads, postcards, stickers—you name it, I probably have it in my journals.

Your designs should resonate with you. Anything can provide you with inspiration for your original designs. Keep your mind and your eyes open—and use a journal to help you remember your inspirations.

Color is probably the most important aspect of my designs. I personally prefer brighter and more saturated hues rather than muted ones. I also love patterns and texture. I sometimes will focus on a color palette and then create from there. Sometimes I'll find a whole group of objects together that looks so appealing just as they are that I just go with it. I did this in the Kseni cake display. It was wonderful just as it was.

My largest challenge in this piece was recreating the glass shelf and the reflections. They had to be correct so that the viewer understood what separated the objects from the background. There were so many colors here that I had to separate each object into its own unit.

Once I created a painting from my photograph, it was easy to transfer it to wool. Instead of worrying about the glass shelf, I just recreated in wool as I saw it. The glass was just the green line in the front. Then I added the reflections and the tiny subtle dark line behind the glass. This was a little more challenging to do in the hooked piece, but I was happy with how close I was able to render it with the wool.

The hooked piece is definitely softer in appearance than the painted one. In the painting, I underpainted the entire scene in black and gray values first, then repainted in color on top. In the rug, it was not possible to do this. So I used different values of hues to create the illusion of the cakes. One long strip of spot-dyed green wool enabled me to create the illusion of the glass shelf. I added white under the main cake in the center helped to define it. If I were to redo this piece, I would use the exact same colors in the wool as in the paints. I think this would help define the objects more clearly.

Kseni Bakery Display
Wool on linen, 24" x 18", 2016

Eric's Candy Apple
Oil on canvas, 36" x 24", 2016

While I was working on my thesis, I also had to fulfill some mandatory painting classes. One assignment was to create a painting inspired by another artist and art movement. I really admired the surrealists like Dali and René Magritte, so Magritte was a natural choice.

René Magritte was a Belgian artist who painted *Le fils de l'homme* (The Son of Man) in 1946. Magritte painted images to question the idea of consciousness and often combined recognizable things used in an unusual way.

I had just ordered candied apples for a thesis project. I asked my son's best friend, Eric, to pose for me with the candy apple in his face. I liked Magritte's use of the landscape background of the ocean and sky, so I appropriated this into my piece—with a modern twist. Instead of the candy apple floating above Eric's face I would have him hold the stick. I painted him exactly as I photographed him, in modern clothing.

I painted this first, then hooked the companion piece. I had a great time playing with colors and values for the candy apple. Even though this piece was not part of my "baked goods" thesis series, I would say this is my favorite and most successful art project.

The painted/hooked background reflects his family's favorite place, Lake Muskoka in Ontario, Canada. In the original Magritte painting, the subject is standing in front of a wall; I decided to paint Eric behind the wall. The hooked portrait was a little more challenging and I had trouble with the blues in the sky. In the end, it did translate well from the painting to the hooking. My professors loved it!

Eric's Candy Apple
Wool on linen, 36" x 24", 2016

CONCLUSION

The most wonderful thing about rug hooking is that there are endless possibilities for creation. We are so lucky to have access to wonderful foundation cloth and tools and fibers to create our own unique textile pieces. It doesn't matter what color palette you prefer or what size strip you like to use in your rugs or hooking. I hope that techniques shared in this book demonstrated how easy it is to prepare your own foundation cloth, and that you will experiment and put your own unique twist on this wonderful and versatile medium.

I hope this book has given you enough instruction and inspiration to create your own rug designs and patterns. This is how I create in wool, but it is not the only way.

My advice to everyone: Take a leap of faith and don't be afraid to experiment!

Baleen Whale, *36" x 24", wool on linen.*
Designed and hooked by Victoria L. Rudolph, 2019.

When I moved to the coast, I wanted to create a large baleen whale rug for my house. I drew out the whale freehand on paper and transferred it onto the linen using red-dot transfer fabric and a lightbox. I had a lot of bright colors in my stash and used these for the whale. I planned the colors for the whale so that some areas would be in shadow and show dimension. I dyed the wool for the water in two shades of aqua to enable me to have lighter and darker areas around the whale.

Look around you, wherever you are. You will find enough inspiration for a lifetime!

ACKNOWLEDGMENTS

When I started rug hooking, I never imagined that I would become part of a larger national community of rug hookers and that I too would be designing my own patterns and teaching both children and adults. Rug hooking has been my passion for almost 15 years. I love learning it, doing it, designing it, teaching it, and meeting other rug hookers. I wouldn't have been able to write this book were it not for the wonderful colleagues, teachers, students young and old, and clients whom I have met along the way.

Steamboat Rug Hookers

I must give credit to my first rug hooking teacher Dixie Coyle. In 2005, I sold my calligraphy and stationery shop turnkey and moved with my husband, two children, Alexander and Olivia, and menagerie of pets to Steamboat Springs, Colorado.

My husband is in the tech business and he had the opportunity to work from home and live in his dream location. Being avid skiers, we unanimously voted to move to Steamboat Springs. This is a little piece of heaven in northern Colorado that boasts some of the world's best skiing. There was only one problem: I had nothing creative to do. Living in a remote town, three hours from the nearest city, there wasn't much need for invitations and calligraphy. The internet had taken over much of this industry, so opening a new shop wasn't going to work.

One day I made my way into our local yarn shop and asked if they might have something for me to learn that didn't require counting or complicated instructions. They directed me to a myriad of rug hooking kits. I purchased a sailboat kit. They told me to try it on my own, as there was no instructor available. I went home, read the instructions, and proceeded to finish the kit in three days. Of course, my loops were full of twists, but I discovered the Zen of pulling up the loops in a rhythmic fashion and I was hooked.

By that autumn, I had purchased and completed four more kits and taken the one class they offered. The shop owner decided I needed to meet Dixie Coyle. Dixie mentored a small hooking group that met in her home rug hooking studio once a month. I joined this group, which she aptly named "Six Times a Hooker," for the six projects we would learn how to do over a six-month period. Six months turned into 12 years. Dixie arranged for several national teachers to come teach workshops, and she was readily available if her students needed help.

When my children started high school, I returned to school to finish my MFA degree. I also began the certification program to become a Pearl K. McGown Certified Instructor in rug hooking.

I dedicate this rug hooking book to Dixie Coyle and the Steamboat Rug Hookers, who became my wooly sisters. We laughed, we dyed wool, we hooked, and we shared many wonderful moments in Dixie's studio and at each other's homes and the Steamboat Springs library.

Here are some others who helped me along the way:

- The Pearl K. McGown crew who have been there for me, through thick and thin.

- Laurie Milne, for being my first new friend in Steamboat and introducing me to the art of rug hooking and convincing me many years ago to "just try it."

- My McGown sisters at the South Central Rug Hooking Teacher's Workshop.

- The ATHA teachers who welcomed me into their classes and encouraged me: Cheryl Bollenbach, Cynthia Norwood, Martha Lowry, Gene Shepherd, and Melissa Pattacini from Honey Bee Hive, who sells some of my patterns.

- Debra Smith, editor of *Rug Hooking* magazine, who encouraged me and believed in this project.

And finally, to my husband Alan and children Alex and Olivia, who have always encouraged me and indulged me in this world of rug hooking. Our house is always filled with strips and bits of wool and other fibers waiting to be looped through a foundation and come to life.

Finally, I want to thank Diane Costello from Fog Dog Studio for taking the photographs for this book. Some of the photographs for project making I took myself, on an iPhone X and iPhone XI. All creations in this book are my original work.

RESOURCES

- *Rug Hooking* magazine, the publisher of this book, five times yearly magazine, filled with interesting articles. It is a great resource for suppliers, teachers, and events. (www.rughookingmagazine.com/)

- Honey Bee Hive (rughook.com/)

- Pearl McGown Teacher Certification Program. Several annual workshops are located around the country. (www.mcgownguild.com/)

- Association of Traditional Hooking Artists (ATHA). For a small fee you can become a member of the largest rug hooking network. They have chapters in most of the United States, and if you don't see a group in your area, you can start one. With your membership you also get a bimonthly magazine. ATHA also holds biennial meetings. (www.atharugs.com/)

BARCELONA RUG TEMPLATE

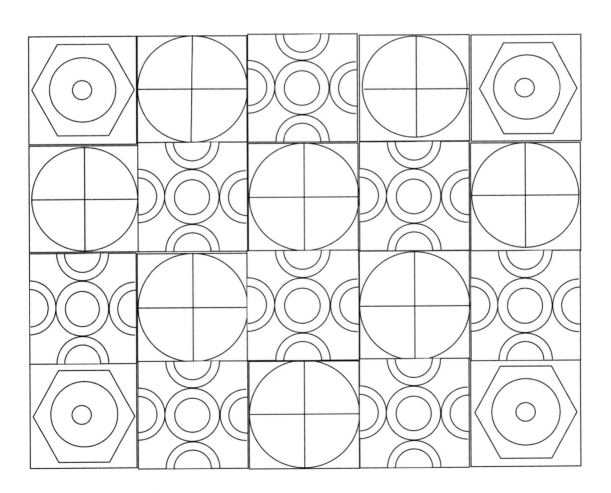

YOU'RE INVITED TO JOIN THE NEW & IMPROVED BOOK CLUB!

Dear Rug Hooker,

If you love *Rug Hooking* Magazine, then you're going to LOVE our new and improved Book Club! We've refreshed our Book Club with even more benefits so that members can maximize their enjoyment of our rug hooking books. Take a peek at the benefits of becoming a member of the NEW *Rug Hooking* Book Club:

- **Guaranteed discounts on new books**

- **Go green! Hassle-free automatic book payments free from pesky paper invoices or postcards**

- **Exclusive monthly discounts on our online store**

- **Secret sales only for book club members**

- **A free E-Newsletter with book club members-only content**

- **Membership is free! No dues, and no membership fees**

Join the new and improved Book Club today to get interesting, informative books just like these for a guaranteed discount.

To learn more about the *Rug Hooking* Book Club and become a Book Club Member today:

 https://www.rughookingmagazine.com/bookclub2021

 877-297-0965 (U.S.)
866-375-8626 (Canada)

Already a Book Club Member?
Click here (or call us) to update your account and access NEW benefits!